I Love to Write!

written by
Jan Mader

Table of Contents

Letter

I wrote a **letter** to Mom. It said, "I love you."

Sign

I wrote a **sign** for my brother. It said, "Stay out!"

Note

I wrote a note to myself. It said, "Don't forget to feed the dog."

9

Card

I wrote a card to Grandma. It said, "I miss you."

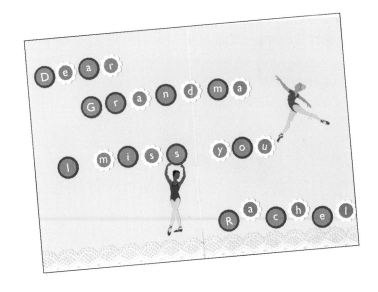

11

Shopping List

I wrote a shopping list. It said, "We need peanut butter and popcorn."

Shopping Lis
We need
peanut butt
and popcorn

13

Cake

I wrote on a cake.
It said, "Happy
Birthday."

Message

I wrote a phone **message** for Dad. It said, "Mr. Dover wants to come over."

Report

I wrote a **report** for my class. My teacher put a gold star on it and hung it on the wall.

Rachel

Her name

...er. She is

...o...e is big.

Email

I wrote an **email** to my friend. It said, "Can you play today?"

Lunch Note

Mom put a note in
my lunch. It said,
"Have a nice day!"

Glossary

email – messages sent and received through an electronic mail system

letter – a direct or personal written or printed message addressed to a person or organization

message – a communication in writing, in speech, or by signals

report – a usually detailed account or statement

sign – a posted command, warning, or direction

Index